Origins

Making Things That Fly

Steph Hughes

OXFORD
UNIVERSITY PRESS

Things that fly

There are lots of things that can fly.
Birds and insects can fly.
Planes and helicopters can fly too.

Can you think of other things that can fly?

This book shows you how to make some things that fly.

Make a paper plane

You can fly your own paper plane. All you need is a sheet of paper!

1 Fold the paper in half.

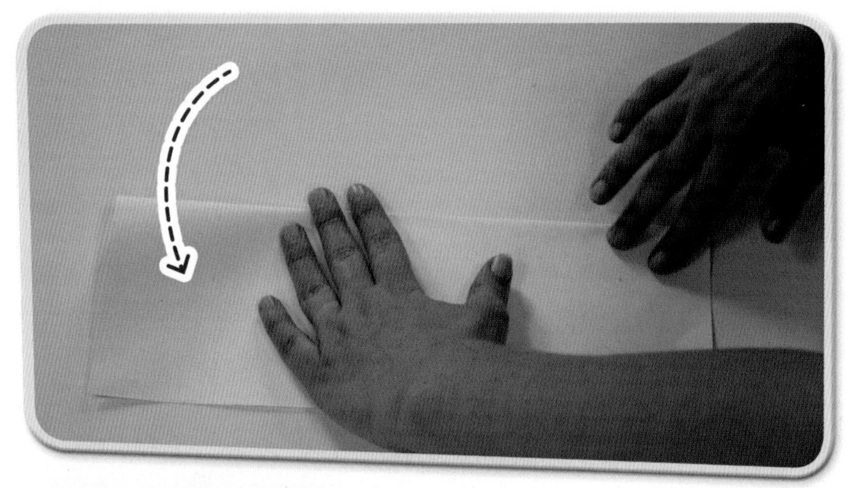

2 Fold the top right-hand corner down. It will make a triangle.

3 Turn the paper over. Do step 2 on the other side.

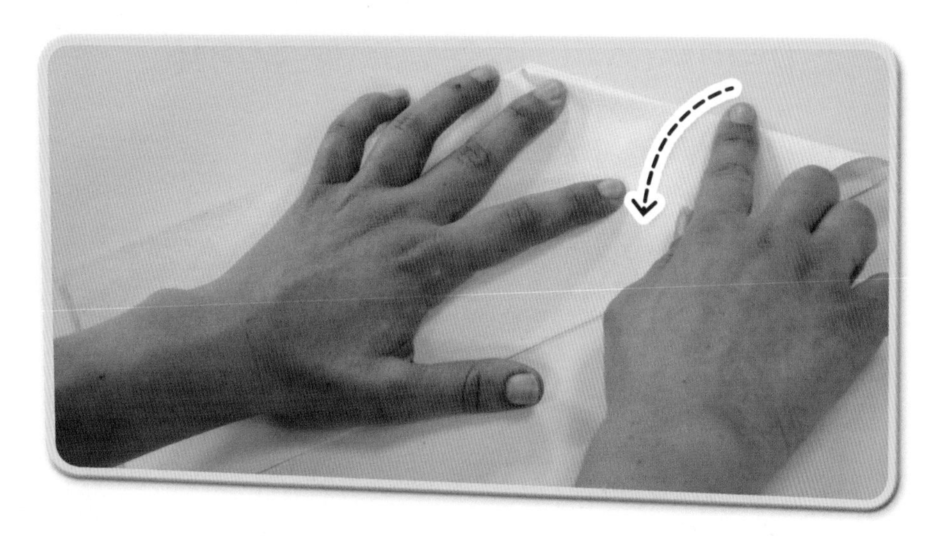

4 Fold down the top corner to the red dot.

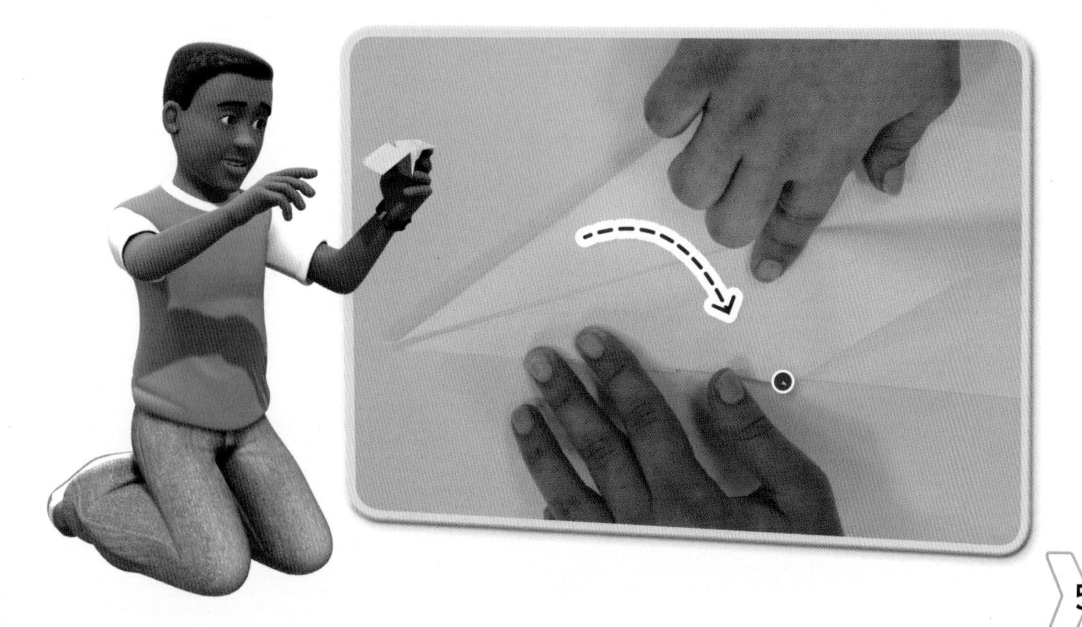

5 Turn the plane over. Do step 4 on this side. Both sides of the plane will look the same.

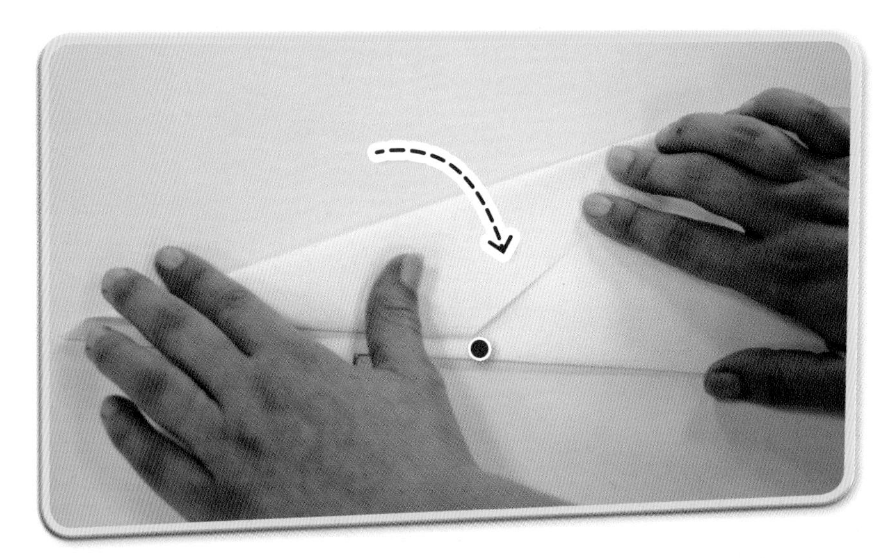

6 Fold down the top corner again to the red dot.

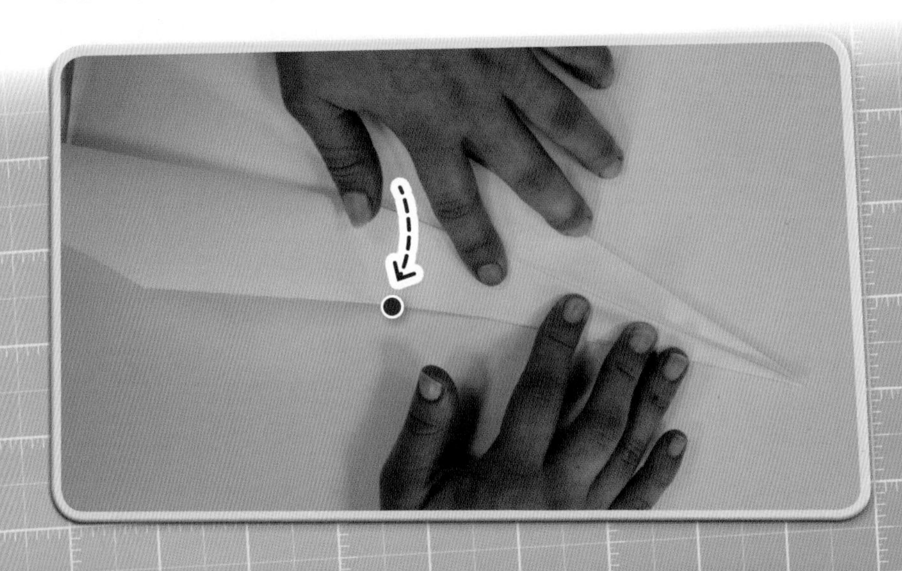

7 Turn the plane over. Do step 6 on this side. Both sides of the plane will look the same.

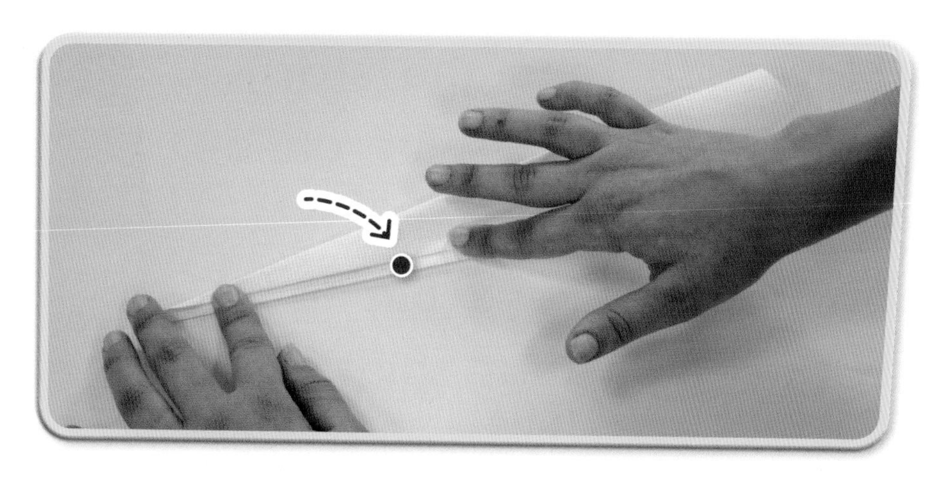

8 Open out the wings. Fly the plane!

Make a roto-copter

Have you read the story *In a Spin*? Ant spins on a sycamore seed.
You can make a paper roto-copter that spins too!

You will need:

sheet of card

paper clip

scissors

1. Cut out a strip of card 17cm by 4cm.

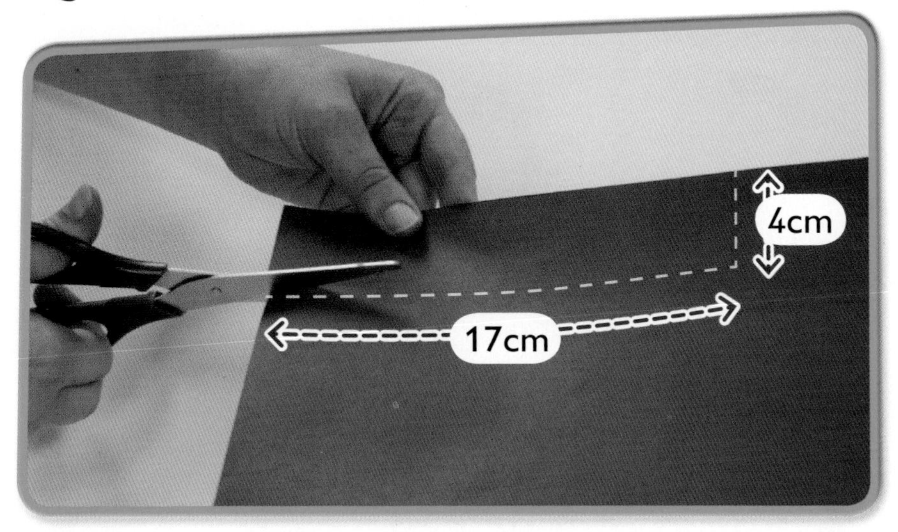

2. Cut a slit halfway up the middle of the strip of paper. This makes the wings.

3 Fold the wings down. Fold one to the left. Fold one to the right.

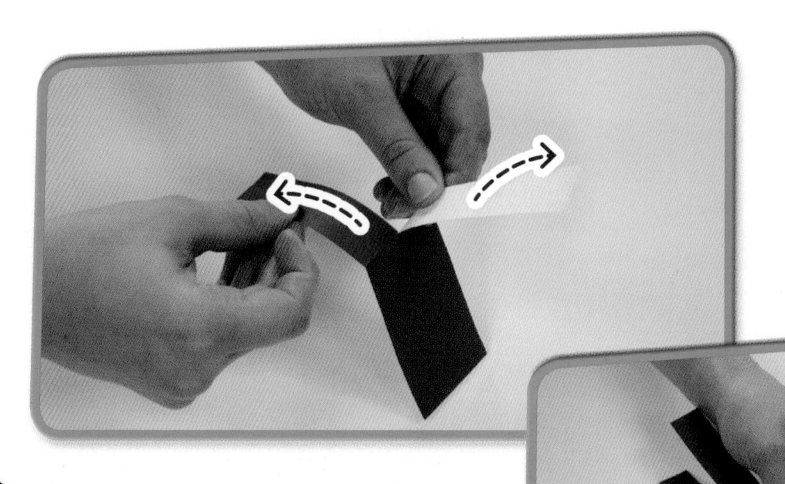

4 Put a paper clip at the bottom of the strip of card.

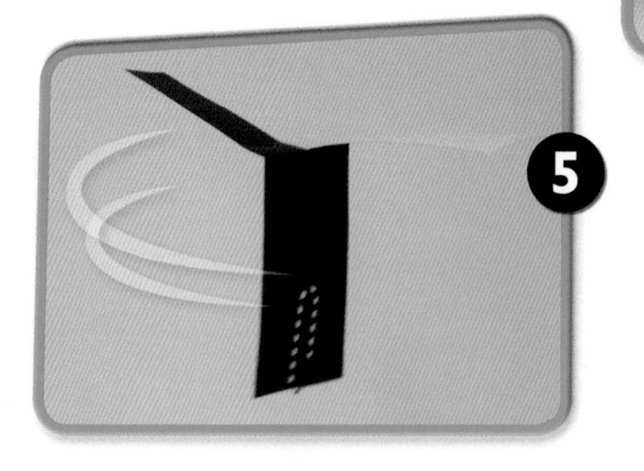

5 Drop the roto-copter. Watch it spin!

You could drop it from different heights. Which height works the best?

Make your own micro-copter

Have you read about the flying machine called the micro-copter yet?
You could make your own micro-copter.

You will need:

feathers

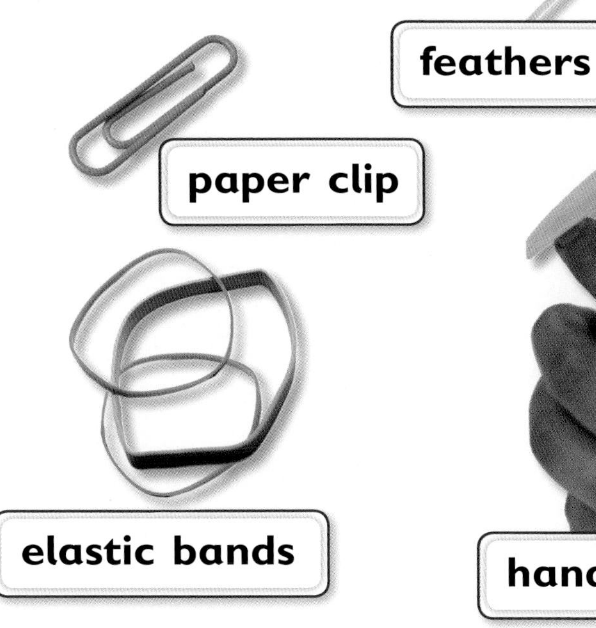

hand fan

Making the wings

1. Hold the hand fan.

2. Tie the feathers to the fan blades. Use elastic bands.

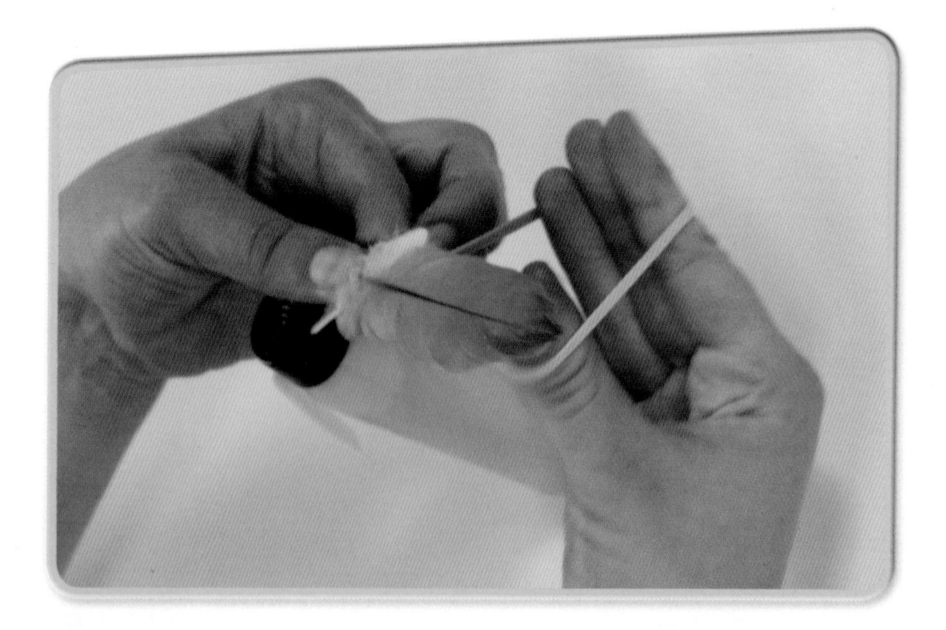

Making the handles

3. Untwist a paper clip.

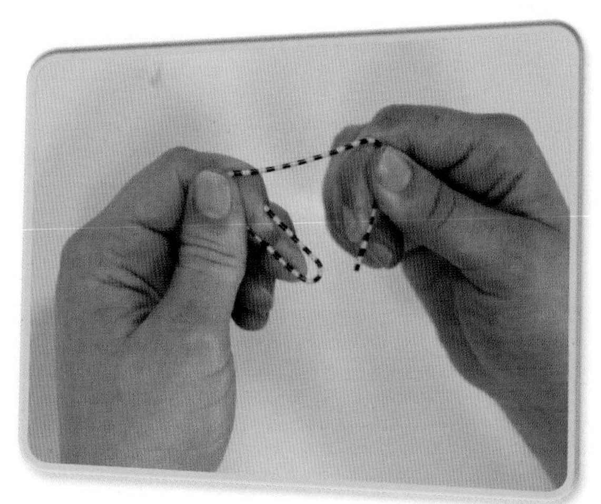

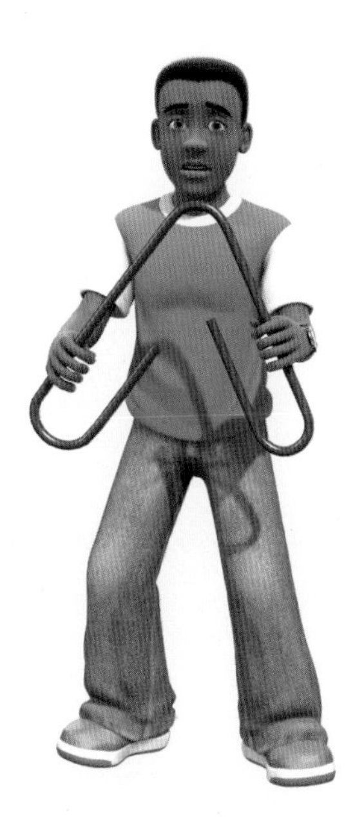

4. Twist the paper clip around the fan. This will make the handles.

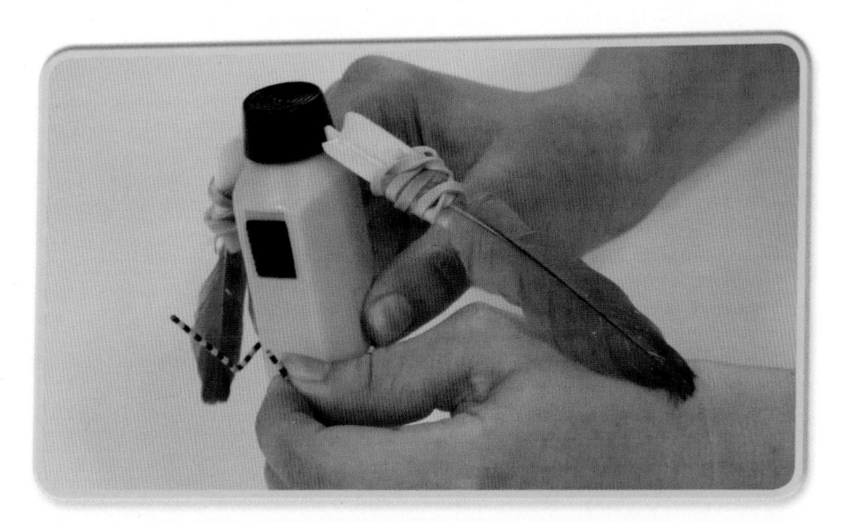

5 Put an elastic band around the fan and the paper clip. This will hold the paper clip in place.

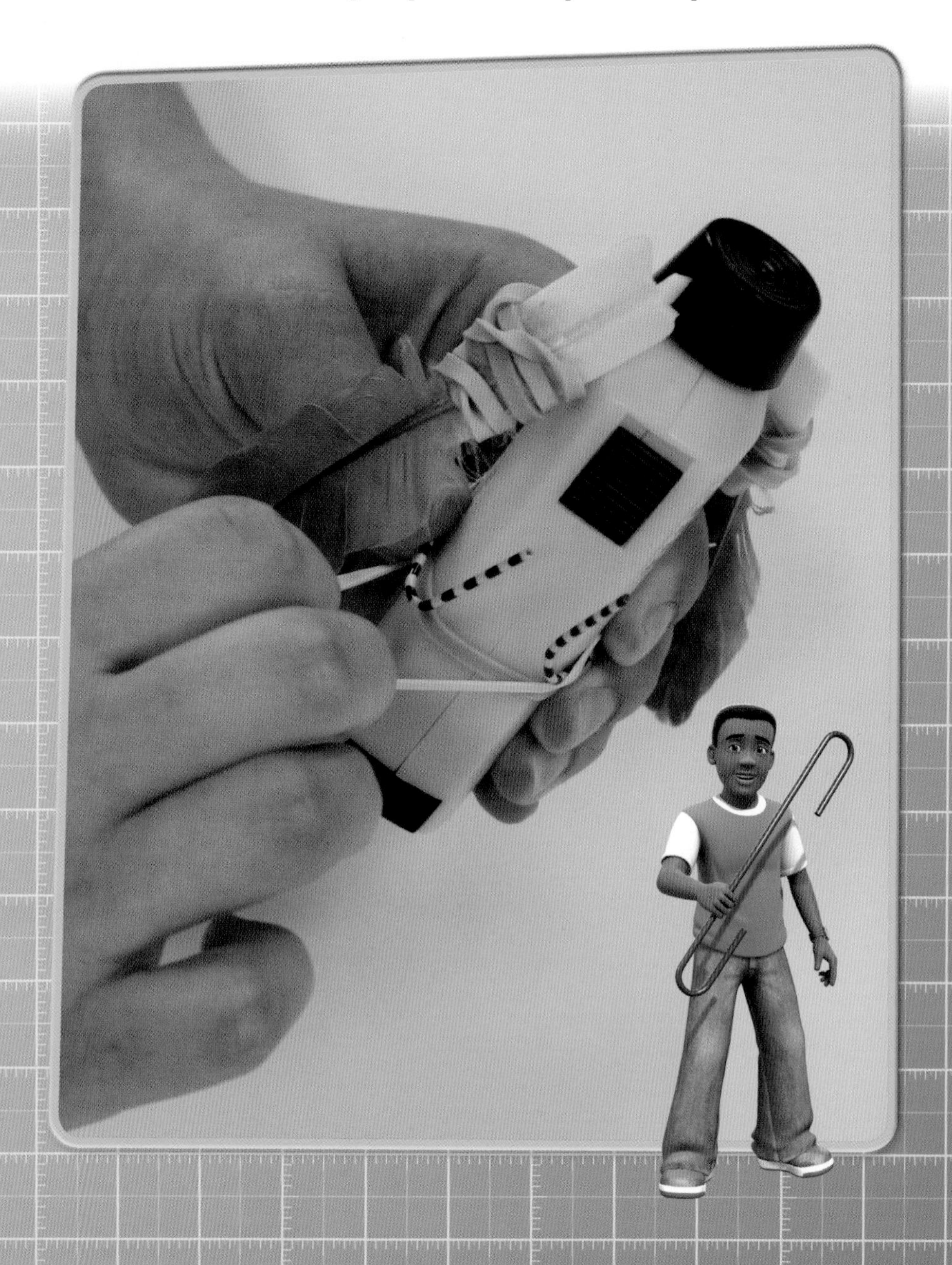

The micro-copter

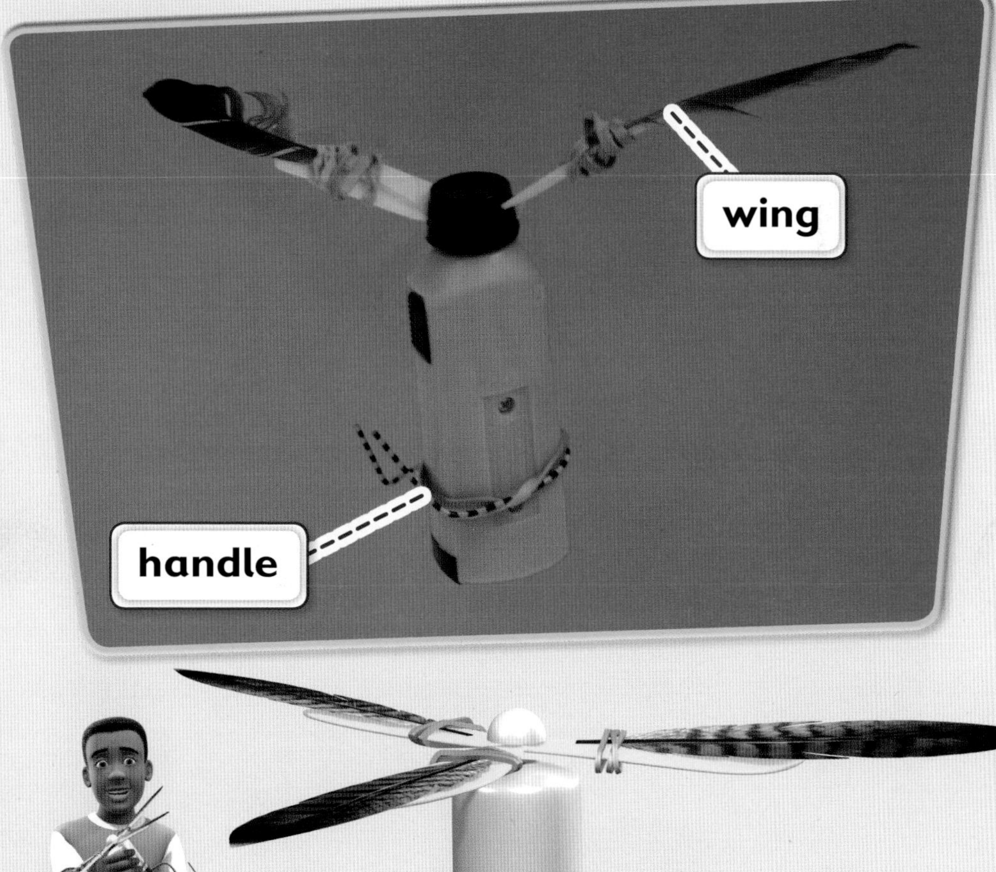

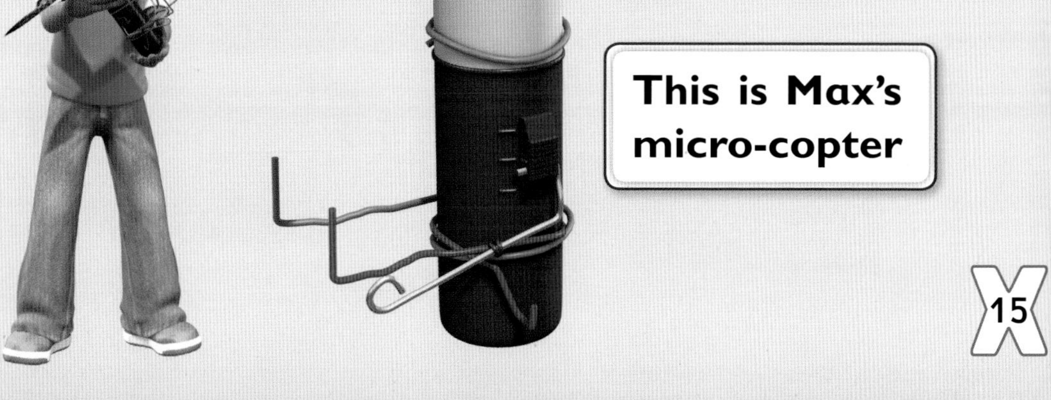

This is Max's micro-copter

Read about a micro-copter adventure …

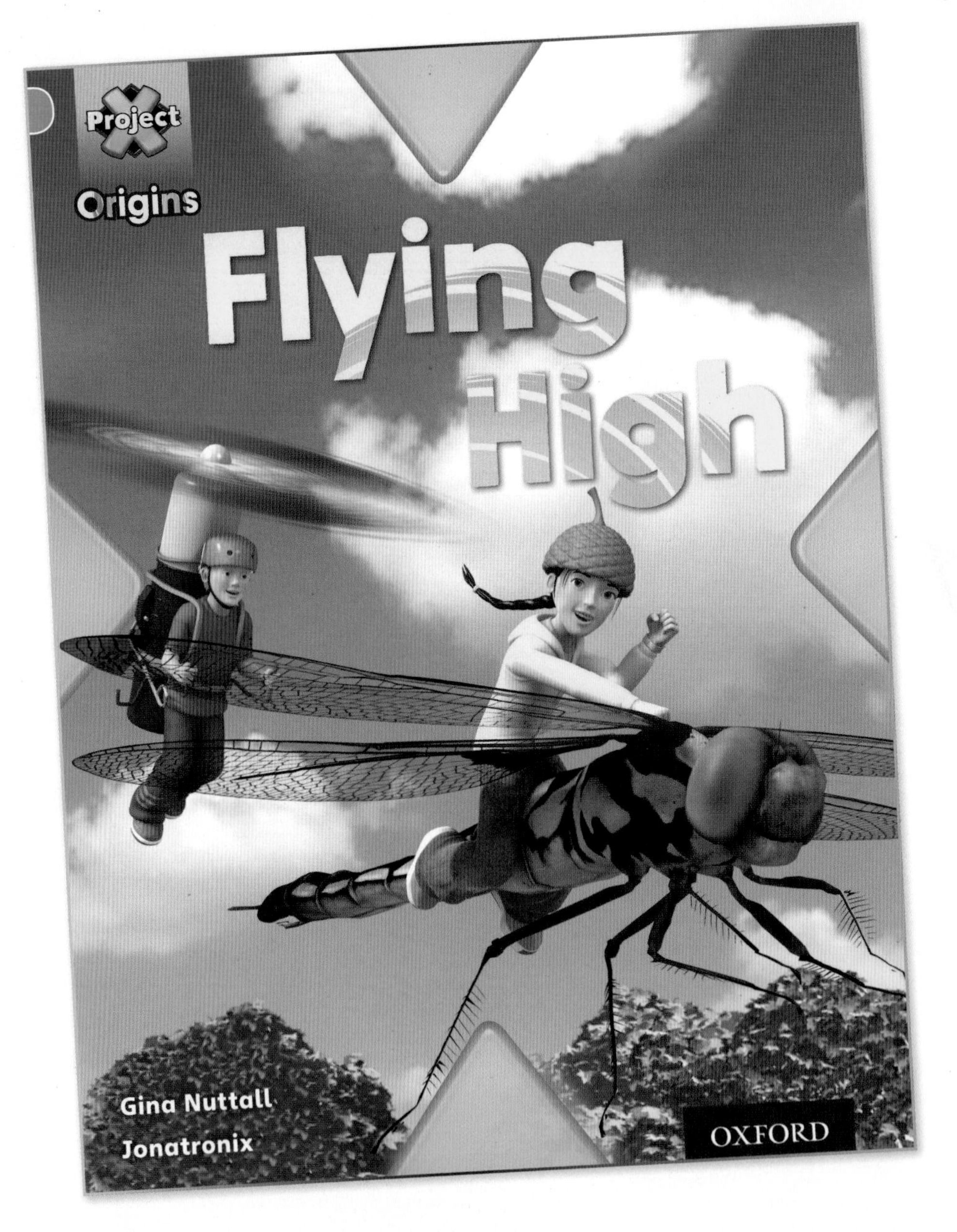